Seattle MARINERS
SAFECO STARS and KINGDOME LEGENDS

TO GENEE, PAUL AND CAL

M's

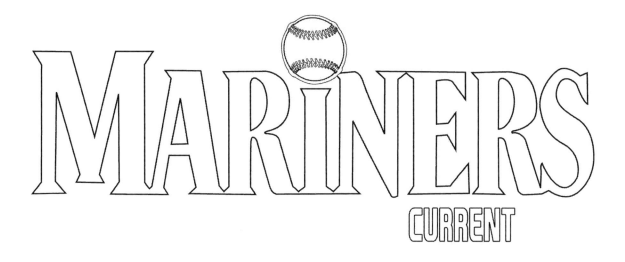

CURRENT

2B
ROBINSON CANO

2016 SEASON STATS

AVG	HR	RBI	RUNS
.298	39	103	107

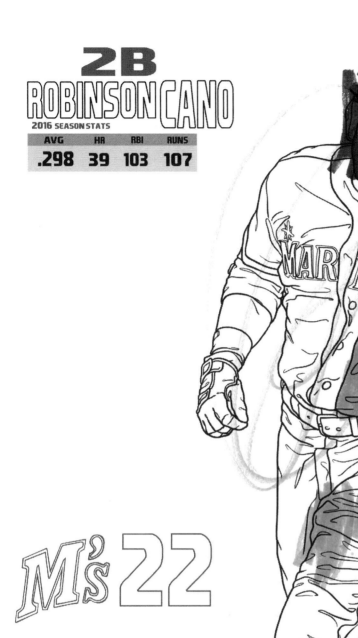

M's 22

BEST SEASON STATS		
2010 PLAYING FOR		Yankees
AB	HITS	BA
626	200	.319
HR	RUNS	RBI
29	103	109
AWARDS / HONORS		
All-Star, Silver Slugger Gold Glove Award		

SP
ARIEL MIRANDA

2016 SEASON STATS

W-L	ERA	SO	SO P/9
5 - 2	3.88	44	6.83

BEST SEASON STATS		
2017	PLAYING FOR	Mariners
GP	IP	ERA
12*	67.1*	3.74*
WIN	LOSS	SO
6*	2*	61*
AWARDS / HONORS		
N/A		

*as of June 2017

M's 37

RF
BEN GAMEL

2016 SEASON STATS

AVG	HR	RBI	RUNS
.188	1	5	9

FIRST **33** GAMES OF

BEST SEASON STATS		
2017 PLAYING FOR Mariners		
AB	HITS	BA
122	38	.325
HR	RUNS	RBI
2	21	16
AWARDS / HONORS		
N/A		

M's 16

M's 52

C

CARLOS RUIZ

2016 SEASON STATS

AVG	HR	RBI	RUNS
.264	3	15	21

BEST SEASON STATS		
2012	PLAYING FOR	Phillies
AB	**HITS**	**BA**
372	121	.325
HR	**RUNS**	**RBI**
16	56	68
AWARDS / HONORS		
All-Star		

1B
DANNY VALENCIA

2016 SEASON STATS

AVG	HR	RBI	RUNS
.287	17	51	72

M's 26

BEST SEASON STATS		
2015	PLAYING FOR	BlueJays
AB	HITS	BA
345	100	.290
HR	RUNS	RBI
18	59	66
AWARDS / HONORS		
N/A		

RP
EDWIN DIAZ
2016 SEASON STATS

SAVES	ERA	SO	SO P/9
18	2.79	88	15.33

BEST SEASON STATS		
2016	PLAYING FOR	Mariners
GP	IP	ERA
49	51.2	2.79
W - L	SV	SO
0 - 4	18	88
AWARDS / HONORS		
N/A		

M's 39

SP
FELIXHERNANDEZ

2016 SEASON STATS

W-L	ERA	SO	SO P/9
11-8	3.82	122	7.16

M's 34

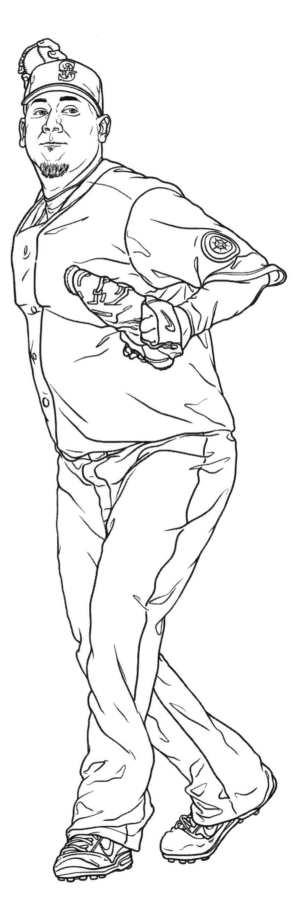

BEST SEASON STATS		
2009	PLAYING FOR	Mariners
GP	IP	ERA
34	238.2	2.49
W - L	SV	SO
19 -5	-	217
AWARDS / HONORS		
All-Star, MLB wins leader		

THE 23RD PERFECT GAME
IN MAJOR LEAGUE HISTORY

On August 15, 2012 Felix pitched a perfect game! Only 22 other players in Major League Baseball history have ever done this!

A perfect game is where a player pitches a victory that lasts at least nine innings and where not one of the other teams players reach a base.

NO HITS, NO WALKS, NO HIT BATTERS

GUILLERMO HEREDIA
2016 SEASON STATS
LF

AVG	HR	RBI	RUNS
.250	1	12	12

M's 5

BEST SEASON STATS		
2017 PLAYING FOR		Mariners
AB	HITS	BA
157*	44*	.280*
HR	RUNS	RBI
4*	19*	10*
AWARDS / HONORS		
N/A		

*as of June 2017

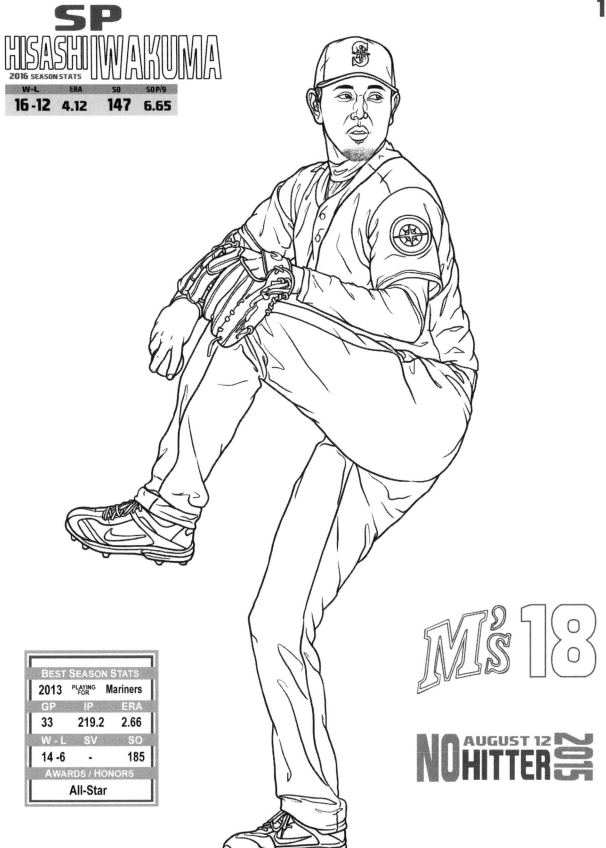

SP
HISASHI IWAKUMA
2016 SEASON STATS

W-L	ERA	SO	SO P/9
16-12	4.12	147	6.65

10

BEST SEASON STATS		
2013	PLAYING FOR	Mariners
GP	IP	ERA
33	219.2	2.66
W - L	SV	SO
14 -6	-	185
AWARDS / HONORS		
All-Star		

M's 18

NO HITTER
AUGUST 12
2015

M's 1

JARROD DYSON
2016 SEASON STATS

AVG	HR	RBI	RUNS
.278	1	25	46

CF

BEST SEASON STATS		
2016	PLAYING FOR	Royals
AB	HITS	BA
299	83	.278
HR	RUNS	RBI
1	46	25
AWARDS / HONORS		
N/A		

SP
JAMES PAXTON
2016 SEASON STATS

W-L	ERA	SO	SO P/9
6-7	3.79	117	8.70

M's
65

BEST SEASON STATS		
2017* PLAYING FOR		Mariners
GP	IP	ERA
10	55.2	3.23
W-L	SV	SO
5 -2	-	62
AWARDS / HONORS		
N/A		

*through June 2017

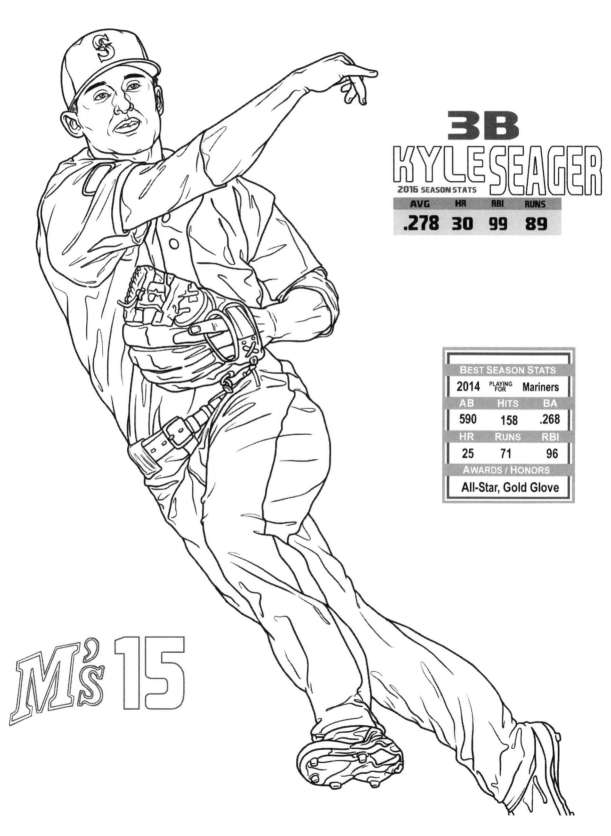

3B
KYLESEAGER

2016 SEASON STATS

AVG	HR	RBI	RUNS
.278	30	99	89

BEST SEASON STATS		
2014 PLAYING FOR		Mariners
AB	HITS	BA
590	158	.268
HR	RUNS	RBI
25	71	96
AWARDS / HONORS		
All-Star, Gold Glove		

M²s 15

C 15
MIKEZUNINO
2016 SEASON STATS

AVG	HR	RBI	RUNS
.207	12	31	16

BEST SEASON STATS		
2014	PLAYING FOR	Mariners
AB	HITS	BA
438	87	.199
HR	RUNS	RBI
22	51	60
AWARDS / HONORS		
N/A		

M's 3

RF
MITCH HANIGER

2016 SEASON STATS

AVG	HR	RBI	RUNS
.229	5	17	9

BEST SEASON STATS		
2017 PLAYING FOR	Mariners	
AB	HITS	BA
79*	27*	.342*
HR	RUNS	RBI
4*	20*	16*
AWARDS / HONORS		
N/A		

*as of June 2017

DH
NELSON CRUZ

2016 SEASON STATS

AVG	HR	RBI	RUNS
.287	43	105	96

BEST SEASON STATS		
2015 PLAYING FOR		Mariners
AB	HITS	BA
590	178	.302
HR	RUNS	RBI
44	90	93
AWARDS / HONORS		
All-Star, Silver Slugger		

M's 23

RP
NICK VINCENT

2016 SEASON STATS

W-L	ERA	SO	SO P/9
4 - 4	3.73	65	9.70

BEST SEASON STATS		
2013	PLAYING FOR	Padres
GP	IP	ERA
45	46.1	2.14
W - L	SV	SO
6 -3	1	49
AWARDS / HONORS		
N/A		

SS
TAYLOR MOTTER

2016 SEASON STATS

AVG	HR	RBI	RUNS
.188	2	9	11

M's 21

BEST SEASON STATS		
2017* PLAYING FOR	Mariners	
AB	HITS	BA
190	38	.200
HR	RUNS	RBI
6	19	22
AWARDS / HONORS		
N/A		

*Through June 2017

SS
ALEX RODRIGUEZ
BEST SEASON STATS

2007	AVG	HR	RBI
	.314	54	156

CAREER		GAMES
1994-2016		2784
TEAM		HPY
YANKEES		$33 MILLION
AB	HITS	BA
10566	3115	.295
HR	RUNS	RBI
696	2021	2086
SB	SO	ERR
329	2287	131

M's Legends

Alex Rodriquez (b. 1975) was born in New York but moved with his parents to the Dominican Republic when he was 4 years old. They later returned to the U.S. and Alex went to high school in Miami, Florida where he was a standout in baseball and football. 1st overall pick in 1993 MLB Draft by the Seattle Mariners. "A-Rod" was a 14-time All-Star selection, a 3x AL MVP, 2x Gold Glove Award winner, 10x Silver Slugger, 5x AL home run leader, 2x MLB RBI leader, MLB batting champ, and World Series Champ ('09).

1B
ALVIN DAVIS
BEST SEASON STATS

1987	AVG	HR	RBI
	.295	29	100

CAREER	GAMES	
1984-1992	1206	
TEAM	HPY	
MARINERS	$1.75 MILLION	
AB	HITS	BA
4240	1189	.280
HR	RUNS	RBI
160	568	683
SB	SO	ERR
7	558	67

M's Legends

Alvin Davis (b. 1960) was born and raised in Riverside, California. He played college baseball at Arizona State University. He made his MLB Debut on April, 11, 1984 for the Seattle Mariners, winning the American League Rookie of the Year Award that same year! Alvin still holds the Mariners record for the most consecutive games reaching base to start a career, with 47. His nickname was "Mr. Mariner," as he was adored by fans.

22

2B
BRET BOONE
BEST SEASON STATS

2001	AVG	HR	RBI
	.331	37	141

Legends

CAREER	GAMES	
1992-2005	1780	
TEAM	HPY	
M's / Reds	$9 MILLION	
AB	HITS	BA
6683	1775	.266
HR	RUNS	RBI
252	927	1021
SB	SO	ERR
94	1295	117

M's

Bret Boone (b. 1969) was born and raised in California. His dad, Bob Boone is a former professional baseball player who played for the Phillies, Reds and the Royals. He later became an MLB manager as well! Bret's unlce and grandpa *also* played professional baseball! Not to mention, that **Brett is also a descendant of the famous pioneer, Daniel Boone!** *Bret became the first-ever third-generation player in MLB history.* He had an excellent career: 3x All-Star, 4x Gold Glove Awards, 2x Silver Slugger Awards, '01 AL RBI leader.

24

C

DAN WILSON

BEST SEASON STATS

1996	AVG	HR	RBI
	.285	18	83

Legends

CAREER		GAMES
1992-2005		1299
TEAM		HPY
MARINERS		$4.5 MILLION
AB	HITS	BA
4186	1097	.262
HR	RUNS	RBI
88	441	519
SB	SO	ERR
23	763	45

Dan Wilson (b. 1969) was born and raised in Barrington, Illinois and began playing baseball at a very young age. He even led his hometown Little League team to a 3rd-place finish in the 1981 Little League World Series! In high school, Dan played both catcher and pitcher. He was drafted in 1987 by the New York Mets, but decided to go to college instead (University of Minnesota). He was later picked 7th overall in the '90 Draft. An excellent defensive player, twice leading league in catching runners stealing. All-Star selection in 1996.

25

3B/DH
EDGAR MARTINEZ
BEST SEASON STATS

1995 AVG	HR	RBI
.356	29	113

CAREER	GAMES	
1987-2004	2055	
TEAM	HPY	
MARINERS	$7 MILLION	
AB	HITS	BA
7213	2247	.312
HR	RUNS	RBI
309	1219	1261
SB	SO	ERR
49	1202	81

Edgar Martinez (b. 1963) was born in New York and is of Puerto Rican descent. In 1982, the Mariners signed Edgar to a minor league contract and he slowly rose in the system until finally making his major league debut on September 12, 1987. He spent his entire professional career in the Mariners organization.
Edgar began his career at third base, but moved to DH after injury. He was a 7X All-Star, 5x Silver Slugger Award winner, 2x AL Batting Champion, AL RBI Leader, Roberto Clemente Award and M's Hall of Fame!

RF
ICHIRO SUZUKI
BEST SEASON STATS

2004	AVG	HR	RBI
	.372	8	60

*still playing

CAREER		GAMES
2001-present		2557
TEAM		HPY
MARINERS		$18 MILLION
AB	HITS	BA
9775	3049	.312
HR	RUNS	RBI
116	1406	767
SB	SO	ERR
508	1061	38

stats through June '17

MLB RECORD
MOST HITS 262 SEASON

Ichiro Suzuki (b. 1973) was born and raised in a small town called Toyoyama, which is in Japan. At the age of seven, Ichiro joined his first baseball team. Ichiro and his father had a daily routine: throwing 50 pitches, fielding 50 outfield and infield balls, and hitting 500 pitches a day! Ichiro Suzuki would go on to become one of the greatest players to ever play the game. 10x All-Star, 10x Gold Glove, 3x Silver Slugger, 2x MLB batting Champ, SB leader, R.O.Y. and AL MVP! 2 MLB Records: Most hits (season), 10x consecutive 200-hit seasons

JAMIE MOYER

P

BEST SEASON STATS

2003 W-L	ERA	SO	SO P/9
21-7	3.27	129	5.40

27

Legends

M's

CAREER		PITCHED
1986-2010		696 GM
TEAM		HPY
MARINERS		$8 MILLION
WINS	LOSS	ERA
269	209	4.25
IP	SHO	SV
4074.0	10	0
SO	SOp/9	NH
2441	5.4	0

Jamie Moyer (b. 1962) was born and raised in Pennsylvania. In high school Jamie played baseball, basketball and golf! He would later attend Saint Joseph's University, where in 1984 he set the school's single-season records in wins (16), earned run average (1.99 ERA) and strikeouts (90). Drafted in 1984, making his MLB debut in 1986, Jamie would go on to have one of the longest professional careers, with 25 seasons! He was pitching when he was 49! MLB All-Star ('03), World Series Champion ('08) and Mariners Hall of Fame!

1996	AVG	HR	RBI
	.271	44	138

CAREER	GAMES
1987-2001	1472

TEAM	HPY
MARINERS	$5.4 MILLION

AB	HITS	BA
5013	1273	.254

HR	RUNS	RBI
310	797	965

SB	SO	ERR
6	1406	33

Jay Buhner (b. 1964) was born in Louisville, Kentucky. His family later moved to Texas and Jay went to Clear Creek High School where he played baseball. He later would go on to play college baseball at McLennan Community College in Waco, Texas. In Jay's freshman season in 1983, McLennan won the junior college World Series. Drafted by the Brave's in 1983. Buhner made a name for himself while with the Mariners, fans adored Jay and his bald head! All-Star (1996), Gold Glove Award Winner and Mariners Hall of Fame!

29

CF
KEN GRIFFEY JR.

BEST SEASON STATS

1997	AVG	HR	RBI
	.304	56	147

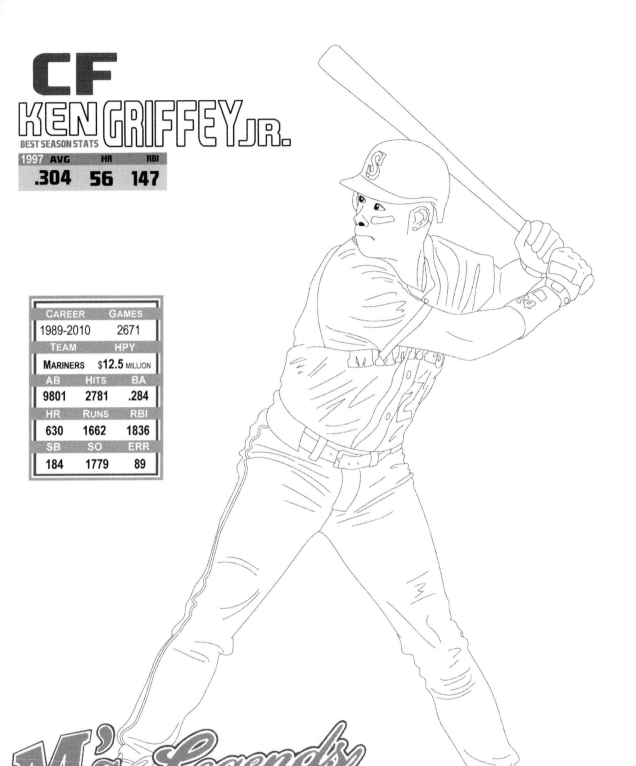

CAREER		GAMES
1989-2010		2671
TEAM		HPY
MARINERS		$12.5 MILLION
AB	HITS	BA
9801	2781	.284
HR	RUNS	RBI
630	1662	1836
SB	SO	ERR
184	1779	89

M's Legends

Ken Griffey Jr. (b. 1969) was born in Pennsylvania but grew up in Cincinnati, Ohio, where his dad, Ken Griffey Sr. played for the Reds. When "Junior" was 6 years old he was in the dugout during Ken Sr.'s back-to-back championships ('75/'76). A superstar at a young age, Junior was the number one pick by the Seattle Mariners in 1987. A 13-time All-Star, AL MVP ('97), 10-time Gold Glove Award winner, 7-time Silver Slugger, 4-time AL home run leader, Mariners retired jersey, Baseball Hall of Fame.

P
MARK LANGSTON
BEST SEASON STATS

1987	W-L	ERA	SO	SO P/9
	19 - 13	3.84	262	8.70

30

NO HITTER APRIL 11 1990
combined

CAREER		PITCHED
1984-1999		457 GM
TEAM		**HPY**
M's / ANGELS		$5 MILLION
WINS	**LOSS**	**ERA**
179	158	3.97
IP	**SHO**	**SV**
2962.2	18	0
SO	**SOp/9**	**NH**
2464	7.5	0

M's Legends

Mark Langston (b. 1960) was born and raised in San Diego, California. He began playing baseball at a young age, and became the star of his high school team. He later went on to play for San Jose State University and was picked by the Mariners in the second round of the 1984 MLB Draft. He began his career the same time as fellow M's Legend Alvin Davis. Davis won AL Rookie of the Year and Mark won Rookie Pitcher of the Year! 3-time AL Strikeout leader, 7-time Gold Glove Award Winner, and a 4-time All-Star!

P
RANDY JOHNSON

BEST SEASON STATS

2001	W-L	ERA	SO	SO P/9
	21 - 6	2.49	372	13.4

CAREER		PITCHED
1988-2009		618 GM
TEAM		**HPY**
MARINERS		$16 MILLION
WINS	**LOSS**	**ERA**
303	166	3.29
IP	**SHO**	**SV**
4135.1	37	2
SO	**SOp/9**	**NH**
4875	10.6	2

M's Legends

Randy Johnson (b. 1963) was born and raised in California. By the time he entered high school, Randy was a star in baseball and basketball. As a senior, he struck out 121 batters in 66 innings! He turned down an offer to go pro and instead went to USC, where he was a teammate of Mark McGwire. His nickname was "The Big Unit," being one of the tallest in MLB history at 6'10". One of the most dominating pitchers of all time. 10x All-Star, W.S. champ, 5x Cy Young, W.S. MVP, Triple Crown, 9x strikeout and 4x ERA leader!

32

MANAGER

LOU PINIELLA

WIN - LOSS RECORDS

CAREER	WIN	LOSS
	1835	1712

with M's	WIN	LOSS
	840	711

63 CAREER EJECTIONS

Legends

M's

Lou Piniella (b. 1943) was born and raised in Tampa, Florida. He loved baseball from the very first time he ever played it, playing American Legion and PONY League baseball. He was a star athlete at Jesuit High School, where he was an All-American *basketball* player! He decided to play baseball in college, attending the University of Tampa, where he was a DII All-American. Lou went on to play 16 years in the MLB, winning 2 World Series championships. Later, as a manager, he would win another. Known for his 'temperament.'

**THE MASCOT
MARINER
MOOSE**

M's
Legends

**SINCE
1990**

MARINERS
LOGOS

MARINERS
DESIGN CENTER

COLOR **M's** JERSEY

41

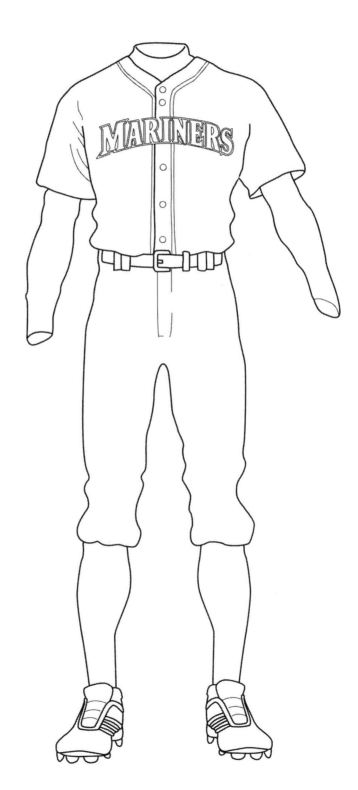

MARINERS

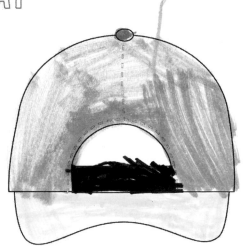
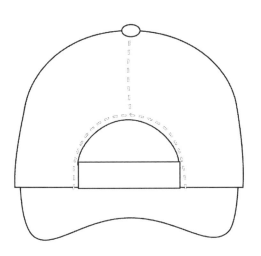

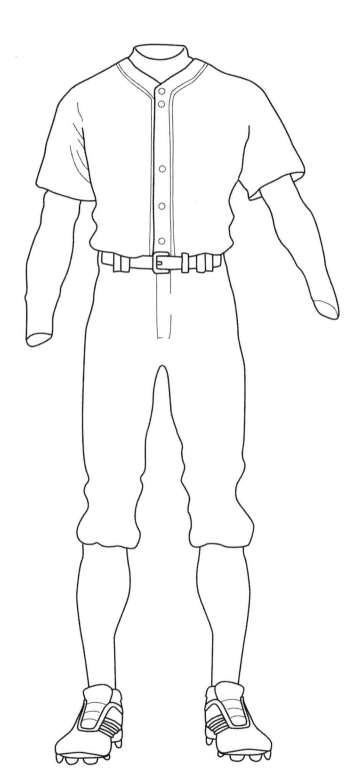

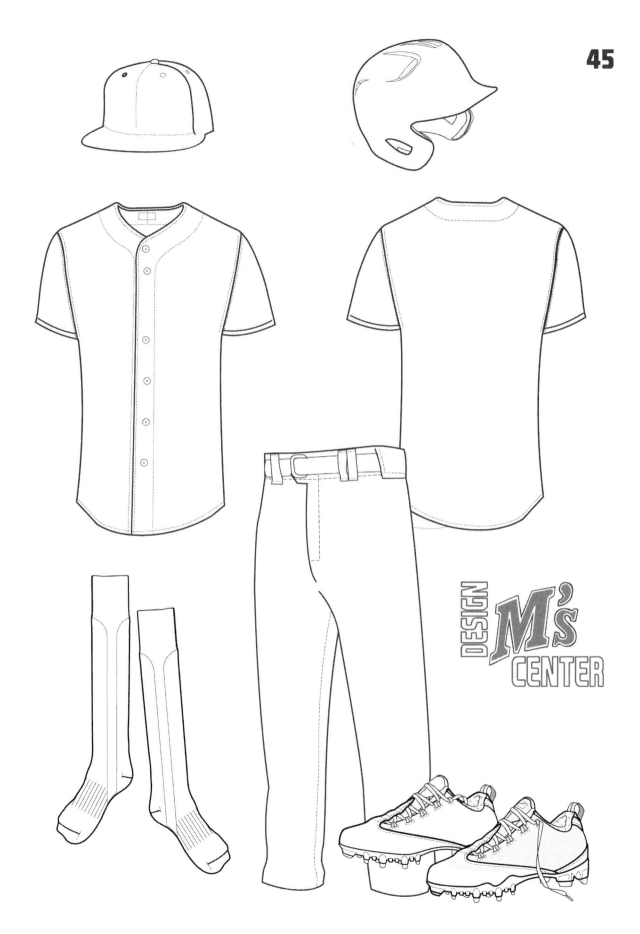

DESIGN M's CENTER

If you enjoyed this book, check out other books by this author:
"Legends of Baseball: Coloring, Activity and Stats Book for Adults and Kids""
-35 Best Series-

Coming Soon:
"Seattle Supersonics Legends""
-35 Best Series-

Made in the USA
Columbia, SC
22 December 2020